# FORMING THE FAITH
## OF
## ADOLESCENTS

# FORMING THE FAITH
# OF
# ADOLESCENTS

Jacques Audinet

*Preface by* Gabriel Moran

HERDER AND HERDER

1968
HERDER AND HERDER, NEW YORK
232 Madison Avenue, New York 10016

Originally published as *Vers une catéchèse des adolescents, essai de méthodologie* by Ligel, Paris, 1964. Translated by E. M. Stewart

© Translation, Geoffrey Chapman Ltd, 1968

*This edition first published* 1968

Nihil obstat: R. D. Georgius Telford, Censor Deputatus
Imprimatur: H. Gibney, Vicarius Generalis
Datum Southwarci die 6a Aprilis 1967

This book is set in Plantin 110, 11 pt on 13 pt
Made and printed in Great Britain

# CONTENTS

# CONTENTS

# Preface

*Gabriel Moran*

It seemed that real progress had been made. The catechetical movement in the first part of this century had been dedicated to the improvement of methods for teaching religion. Then in the thirties the work of Josef Jungmann came like a crashing blow. It challenged the presuppositions on which the movement had been built. Our problem, Jungmann charged, is not we cannot get our message across, but that we do not know what the message is. The root difficulty is the content of the message itself.

The post-Jungmannian could thus be identified by his motto: the real problem is not method but content. From that first third of the century when "they kept breathing over dry bones in the valley but the fallen did not rise" (Sloyan), we had moved to the second third of the century when the announcement of the glad tidings of salvation was to have primacy. This was progress indeed. The remaining task seemed to be the dissemination and clarification of the rediscovered content, the core of the Christian message.

Something is still nagging us, however. As we enter the last third of this uproarious century we are vaguely aware of something basically wrong. We sense that there is more needed than the perfecting of the details of the new content. Even when the curricula are well nourished by the best content available, there is uneasiness on the part of teachers. This dissatisfaction is not traceable simply to impatience for concrete or sensational results. There are fundamental questions which still need asking because such questions are never fully resolved. The great scholars of the past have not answered our questions and they would be the first to admit it. We respect the work of a great man like Jungmann not by repeating what he said in the thirties but by asking the same kind of questions as we face our own future. The lines of future directions in religious education have perhaps begun to emerge in the last few years.

The present book by the distinguished professor, Jacques Audinet, is a modest but significant contribution to the emerging era. It is a book about method. Before the reader stops here with the thought that this is where he came in, it must be immediately added that there is no reversion here to an earlier era of methodological questions. Instead, there is a claim that the coming era will be one very much concerned with method but method now understood in a much more sophisticated fashion. In a movement such as this one it is temptingly simple but grossly erroneous to use the image of a pendulum swinging back and forth. People who think in scattered pieces are always looking for that proper balance that combines extremes. The real thrust into the future has little to do with pendulums at all. Rather the forward movement is the one that is characterized by greater depth, integrity and inner coherence.

To think of the present stage as the addition of a little more method to the reformed content would be to miss the significance of the entire movement. The question is not whether to emphasize content or method but what is their inner relationship in human life and in Christian faith. Strange as it may seem, this is a novel question as, for example, the "probings" of a Marshall McLuhan have revealed. What was wrong with an emphasis upon content in catechetics was the assumption that there is a content to Christianity apart from a style of communication. In the coming era the catechist is going to have to listen to the communication theorist and the organizational expert as well as to the sociologist and the psychologist. The theology that is alive and growing will not only accept but reinforce this concern for the media of communicating, the manner of thinking, and the style of living.

It must be admitted that the word *method* is perhaps unsalvageable from its inglorious history. In catechetical literature it is a word long associated with gimmicks and tricks to sneak over the message. For this reason, Audinet decides on the word *approach* rather than method. At least in English, this substitute word is also inadequate for the rich and complex meaning suggested above. However, the term is adequate for the specific task of the author in these essays. He asks us to consider a few approaches to the religious education of adolescents. The temptation for the reader will be to fix the author's outlined approaches into a set pattern or developed system. For example, the third way seems almost to be a synthesis of the first and second. The author warns us to avoid such hasty conclusions. His three approaches are simply that: three ways of teaching that may be variously used, combined or omitted.

American teachers will probably find this kind of catechetical development congenial to their own thinking. The authors are less sure of themselves but more realistic, less apt to inject the good news which solves adolescent problems but more attentive to the questions, desires, and ideals which are already present in adolescent lives. There are few answers for the teachers to have secured beforehand, but there is strong encouragement for teachers to follow their own heads and hearts. Audinet maintains that one cannot predetermine exactly what should be taught or what results should be expected. One can only hope that by "evocative descriptions" he might contribute to the adolescents coming to a deeper understanding of their own lives.

Whatever the theoretical deficiencies of American catechetics, it has never lost contact with a tradition that is soaked in concern for practicality, experience and liberty. This last, the value of freedom or liberty, Audinet is particularly attentive to. Most of his second approach is centered on this point. He repeatedly condemns any use of "blackmail" or any raising of false hopes. He is aware that the teaching of adolescents has often been affected by subtle threats. These techniques of coercion have now become more covert but for that very reason more inhuman. The catechetical movement, despite all its talk about freedom in Christ, has not divested itself of manipulative tendencies.

Underlying the approaches of Audinet is a Christian vision in which theology and anthropology are inseparable. The author has not the space to develop this theoretical foundation. He adverts to it only in a footnote. It is a point, nevertheless, that must be noticed. The advocacy of dealing with the situation of one's hearers could be misunderstood as a reductionist movement in which Christianity is exchanged for the latest fads. It should instead be seen as a plea for adult teachers who have so integrated Christian faith into their lives that they can speak with rich simplicity and non-technical profundity. This kind of teacher possessing adequate theological preparation can speak relevant to the situation without watering down the

Christian faith. This kind of teacher, it may be added, is not produced in sixty day courses.

At the end of this work we find ourselves still left with a sketch. Audinet knows as well as anyone that French writers cannot demonstrate how to teach American adolescents. He is wise enough to refrain from attempting a universal programme. He points out that there are great differences in theorizing on the catechesis of small children as compared to that of the adolescent. In the case of the former he believes that the pattern is fairly simple and stable. With adolescents, on the other hand, the variables of time and place cause a fantastic complexty. It thus becomes almost impossible to make any universal conclusions or to lay down any set rules of procedure.

Tentative and unsystematic insights are all that one can demand in a book of this kind. The reader must fill in his own details. In the United States extensive secular study has been done on adolescent development. For the most part this rich store of information has not been incorporated into religious education. In addition the American school system has made available a fund of teaching experience with adolescents. There has not been enough appreciation of the value of this almost unique experience. Audinet's book will be worthwhile if it does nothing more than give us the impulse to trust in our own experience and to integrate secular learning into our attempts at catechizing adolescents.

# Foreword

*Sister Margaret of Jesus DHG*

In 1960 an international conference of leaders of the catechetical movement assembled at Eichstätt elaborated the principles of catechesis in a formula which has since remained unchallenged. The purpose of all catechesis is to effect an encounter between man in the existential situation of a sinful world, and the message of God's love expressed and effected in Christ. This message of God's loving and saving purpose comes to us in the twentieth century through a four-fold mediation: bible, liturgy, doctrine and Christian witness.

A perceptive observer of the catechetical scene during recent years, however, might well detect a certain development with regard to the last-named of these "four ways". Originally "Christian witness" was taken to mean the witness of Christian living in the lives of the saints, in the history of the Church; the great exemplars of Christian living showed forth in their lives the values and the virtues of the Gospel, and Christ is seen to live on in his saints. Very quickly, however, it was realized that even secular events can in their turn be seen to bear witness to Christ, can be effective in making meaningful to us the reality of God's saving purpose, whenever they call into question the deeper issues of life. And so we spoke, not so much of "catechesis from Christian witness" as of "catechesis from life witness". A conviction that there is in fact no catechesis unless there is encounter between the word of God and the real-life situation of the child led to a deeper development. Teachers of adolescents in particular were driven by their understanding of their young people to go even further. The mystery of salvation is, we know, relevant to life; but it must be perceived as relevant by our adolescents. It is precisely the seeming irrelevance of religion to a materialistic and increasingly autonomous society which appears to the chief obstacle preventing God's word from finding an echo in the hearts of young people today. We need a catechesis which will spring from the life-experience of the young, not as a gimmick to titivate an ephemeral interest, but as a genuine experience, shared by teacher and taught, which will bring to the consciousness of the adolescent the essential human situation of which he is by now confusedly and inarticulately aware. This is what we call a "catechesis from life experience".

While practising teachers were being led by reflection on their daily work to experiment in this approach to catechesis, theologians were indirectly supplying its theoretical justification. The growing realization in contemporary theology of the significance and implications of the mystery of the incarnation has an immediate relevance to the catechetical problem. If by virtue of the incarnation there is nothing in human experience to which Christ is a stranger, then there is nothing in human experience which cannot be a way to him.

"The whole of man's world is expressive of God's revelation in Christ. Nothing of itself is guaranteed to be a revelatory instrument, but everything by the grace of God has become capable of being revelatory of the Christian God. This fact opens unlimited possibilities for the teaching of the Christian revelation."[1]

Father Jacques Audinet is in the front rank of those practising catechists who, realizing both the theological and the psychological justification for a catechesis from life experience, have for some time been exploring these possibilities. Working with teams of students at the Catholic Institute in Paris, he has tried out in the classroom various forms of such a catechesis, and this book is an analysis of and a reflection upon his experience. The difficulties of such an approach are not glossed over; readers who are also teachers will recognize their own adolescent pupils in its pages:

"We speak to them of their problems, and all good text books have chapters on matters like the relationships between boys and girls, friendship, or the work of Christians in the world. Why then is it that we so often have the feeling that it is all to no avail? To the ones that listen it is just a matter of words, lifeless, distant words, while deep down within them the passionate love of life continues to grow, unmoved by our words, which seem quite beside the point . . ." (p. 72).

Father Audinet's sensitivity to the adolescent betrays him in the pages from which I quote into an eloquent warmth of style which is not habitual. For the most part this little book is written with an almost clinical sobriety, an analytic approach which distinguishes for the sake of analysis elements which in practice would be fused. The many teachers who are

[1] Gabriel Moran, *God Still Speaks*, London and New York, 1967.

already experimenting in this field will welcome a reflection which will serve as catalyst to their own experience; while teachers who have perhaps been deterred hitherto by the rather amorphous character of this most valuable catechetical approach will be encouraged to try, by the logical structures which this book provides.

Chapter One

# What is the catechetical approach?

All genuine catechesis should pass on the message of Christ, who is both truth and life. This message must be "known", but we must remember that this knowledge is a "knowledge of faith".

This essay is a study of method. Here the first question asked by the catechist concerns the process by which an adolescent can come to a knowledge of faith. Exactly how does faith fit into the adolescent's picture of the world?

That is what we are going to find out in this chapter.

## I. WHERE SHOULD WE START?

(a) Anyone who has to give religious instruction to adolescents, whether he is a teacher, a chaplain or anyone else, cannot escape a feeling of anxiety as he prepares to face his class. "Am I going to get through to them?" Whatever his talents, however great his authority and however conscientious his preparations, there remains a feeling of uncertainty.

The attention or interest of the group does not depend only on the techniques used, but on things that seem to escape definition and any carefully thought out preparation. At this point religious education is in danger of becoming a matter of chance. Success will be welcomed because it helps the faith, and failure will be admitted with regret: "It didn't work. . . ."

But what is a catechesis that "works"? And who can tell whether it is "successful"? Is success to be judged merely from appearances?[1] It is this preoccupation with immediate results that so often turns our catechesis from its true direction.

(b) In many of the current books written for the religious education of adolescents one can actually see a discrepancy between the starting-point for the lesson and the actual presentation of the message. As a rule the introduction is carefully prepared and developed, for the catechist is anxious to arouse interest. To do this he takes great care in the choice of teaching aids (questionnaires, projects, details from actual life, documentary material of all sorts). In comparison with this, the presentation of the message that follows seems flat and lifeless. Even if it is intellectually sound, it seems to lack the consistency and the real appeal of the introduction.

It all looks as though, in the first stage, the catechist is trying to get his class moving (rather like a runner getting

---

[1] Only God knows the secret of men's hearts. It is impossible for us to judge the real success of any catechesis, for that is God's secret. There are however certain signs that the catechist can look for (atmosphere, feeling of sincerity, deep interest in the demands of the message, etc.), which allow him to judge the catechesis. But such signs are a result. If they are sought in themselves, the interest and atmosphere which they create can ruin the catechesis.

into his stride), so that in the second stage he can make use of the speed acquired to carry them through to the level of the knowledge of faith (just like taking an obstacle "in one's stride").

Unfortunately experience shows that this rarely happens. The obstacle (in this case the knowledge of faith) remains an obstacle. The class ceases to feel interested and the catechist, like an unsuccessful coach, feels disappointed with his difficult pupils and their lack of interest in the Christian message.

(c) But is it not rather the method that should be blamed? The expression "to get over the Christian message" carries its own condemnation. The jockey has to get his horse over the obstacle. But tricks will never help people to reach a knowledge of the faith.

If we must speak of "getting across" the message of faith, let us do so with misgivings. For our part we prefer to speak of an "approach" when we describe that movement of encounter between the young person and God's plan, for this is what our teaching must bring about.[1]

## 2. AN ATTEMPT AT A DEFINITION

We could define this catechetical "approach" in this way:

"The catechetical approach is the movement by which God's designs are put before the person in relation to his outlook on the world, his expectations and needs."

We shall now try to explain the meaning of the three key ideas in this definition.

---

[1] We prefer the word "approach" to "method". This latter term suggests a number of proceedings quite external to the message and to the person concerned. Furthermore it does not take account of the "dynamic" character of teaching adolescents. One could say the same of some of the other expressions sometimes used. But the word "approach" suggests dynamism, and it shows much better how the whole point of the catechesis is to allow the young person to meet the initiative of God as he reveals himself.

(a) *It is a question of movement.* As in every act of know-ledge, one starts from things better known, or more distant. This "getting across", of which we have just spoken, is then a sort of journey. It is a question of relating known facts to those not so well known. Now the grace of faith does not suppress this movement in our minds, this *cogitatio*, which is part of all knowledge (at least normally), and the first task of our teaching is to make this easy. What catechesis must do is to bring about this knowledge of faith in the adolescent in the form of a movement, of a step taken.

But we must not forget that it is a knowledge of faith, and this means a knowledge that relates the whole person receiving this grace to the whole of God's plan revealed to him.

(b) *This plan of God is revealed.* That means it is given to us. Only the whole of God's plan can be regarded as the object of this knowledge of faith. In fact this is an extremely simple reality (to believe is to believe in Jesus Christ) and yet at the same time diverse and complex, since it comes to us through sacred history, the liturgy and the secular thought of the Church.

With adolescents more than any other age-group it is essential to make this unity stand out amid all the variety of knowledge handed down by Christian culture. At the background of all our courses and programmes the face of Christ must be seen. Whatever the subject, the aim of this catechetical approach will be this simple manifestation of God's plan in Jesus Christ.

But one term leads to another. This movement towards Christ is the act of a person, in this case an adolescent. What does it mean for an adolescent "to know"?

(c) *The adolescent's way of looking at the world.* This is the age when the first suggestions of an adult view of the world begin to appear. But efforts at rational thought are still rather confused by emotion. This confusion is only overcome by fits and starts and soon returns. It is more difficult than at any other age to separate ideas from values, desires and experiences. The complex nature of this discovery of the world cannot be ignored by the movement of knowledge (even knowledge of faith). It is in the midst of this confusion and these moments of clarity that the catechist must reveal the face of Christ.

So the movement of religious teaching must take into account all these aspects of an adolescent's knowledge, his whole way of discovering the world, everything in him that is unfulfilled, even transitory. For this is how his personality is. The second pole of our teaching then is the young person's way of looking at the world, all his hopes and needs.

This approach will be a constant alternation between this way of looking at the world, these hopes and needs on the one hand, and the face of Christ on the other.

This movement will guide the whole of religious teaching: the plan of the course, the choice of texts and personal testimonies, the presentation of illustrations and archeological details, all the different activities that can find their place in a religious course, the procedures used, enquiries, questionnaires, etc., all this is only aimed at bringing about this meeting between Jesus Christ and the young person, and making this step, which is the knowledge of faith, easy for him.

A description of the different types of approach to the knowledge of faith at adolescence will thus allow the teacher to see what it is that holds his teaching together. For is it not true that the catechist is often disturbed when he reads about all the schemes and activities put forward in the various programmes? With implicit trust in "the people who have thought the whole thing out", he is frequently content simply to adopt the various suggestions made. In this way the catechesis resembles a puzzle and the catechist (and of course his class) cannot see the general pattern, because he has not grasped what gives unity to all these diverse elements, namely the processes of the adolescent's knowledge of faith.

Our object is to try to describe these processes in a concrete fashion and in their various forms, in other words to describe the various teaching approaches in adolescent catechesis.

## 3. ANOTHER DIFFICULTY

The problem is whether this is at all possible.

(a) In the case of children it is quite easy to give a description of the teaching approach. The child is stable and the processes of its thought are known. Without too much difficulty the careful catechist will be able to imagine how the child looks at the world. So it becomes easy for him to anticipate the course of a lesson.

For many years now, in the training colleges and all the books and reviews dealing with the subject, the elements of this simple approach have been put forward in a way that has become traditional. Apart from the variations proper to each author, a common approach can be discerned. Gaining the attention of the class, presentation of revelation and its development, prayer, etc., are the elements of the teaching approach that is suitable for children. This is something that can be understood. And from this fact it has been possible to make advances in the study of method in the teaching of children.

(b) But in the case of the adolescent things are not so simple. And the impression we have today that no real progress is being made probably comes to some extent from this difficulty in understanding quite so clearly the approaches proper to adolescent catechesis. In fact the view the adolescent has of the world is far more fluid and dependent on the immediate moment than the child's. The processes of an adolescent's thought simply escape the educator, and many refuse to venture on to such uncertain ground as that of a young person's interests and, as far as teaching the faith is concerned, prefer to remain on the firm ground of well-tried doctrinal formulas. They have recourse to a text-book and give their class teaching which is certainly solid but often lacking in interest for those who have to undergo it. The content is no doubt rich, but, because it is not presented in a way that follows the process of a young person's knowledge and according to an appropriate approach, the result is simply boredom and the pupils do their best to suffer from it as little as possible.[1]

Is it then at all possible to aim at a description of the approaches to a knowledge of faith in adolescents?

(c) Experience shows that description is indeed difficult. Several descriptions are necessary, since the actual development will differ according to the gifts of each teacher. Any catechist will find it hard to describe his method: even though he knows his class and is master of his subject he will constantly have to introduce and accept things that were not foreseen. Questions, digressions and repetitions will follow one another, so that a graph of a religious class with adolescents would show a very irregular curve. The points where the religious message in the strictest sense is being conveyed will stand out less, but who can say that faith is not involved even at what appear to be the lowest points on the curve?

(d) If this curve cannot really be described it may be possible at least to find the formula (to continue the mathe-

---

[1] The catechists who have tried to transfer to adolescent teaching the simple approach suited to small children have found it a waste of effort. This is also the reason for using different terms when speaking of religious education of adolescents.

matical analogy). What is needed here—more than the sort of detailed description that can be given of the simple approach suited to children – seems to be an analysis, with a view to finding out the various types of approach to knowledge proper to adolescence. What are the different types of approach that make it possible to relate all the realities of the life and knowledge of the young to the message of Jesus Christ, without being false to either these realities or the message?

We are going to attempt this analysis and in each of the types mentioned we are going to point out the basic elements, the way of putting them into practice from the point of view of teaching, and also the risks of "betrayal" that are possible, which means the difficulties peculiar to each type in relation to a knowledge of faith.

It is wise to admit at once that such a procedure is bound to be to some extent artificial, for the various approaches that we shall mention one after the other are in reality often more or less combined. It can even be said that it is the passage from one to another that makes any catechesis really rich and satisfying, for the interest of the young is often held by passing from one type of thought to another. The catechist must be aware of this, so that he can make full use of all the possibilities at his disposal.

On the other hand such a procedure does allow us to make a fairly wide-ranging study of the various possibilities open to teachers, while at the same time it helps to show what it is in each type of approach that allows the passage from the level of the questions or the expectations of the young people to the level of faith. It helps to show the turning-point, the precise point on which any progress in the knowledge of faith depends.

Chapter Two

# The first approach:
# the rational approach to the subject
# seen as a problem

The rational approach to the subject seen as a problem—this description may well surprise the reader, since for some years anything qualified as "rational" or "notional" has been viewed with a certain suspicion by catechists.

However, this is not what we mean here when we speak of a rational approach. And if it is mentioned in the first place, this does not mean that it is considered more or less important than the others. It is quite simply that it seems to us to be one of the ways of religious knowledge among adolescents. We do not therefore intend to leave it undiscussed, nor do we wish to make it seem more important than it is. We must look for its possibilities and its limits, and from these we can judge the conditions for its use.

## 1. WHAT IS THIS APPROACH?

(a) An example will show this more easily. Imagine a

B

course in the sixth form on "the Church and the unity of the world".[1] The plan of this course might be as follows:

Introduction: the unity of the world, what does that mean?
—efforts towards unity;
—signs of division.
Question: Why are these efforts made? Why do they succeed or fail? How can the Church bring about unity in the world?
The Christian answer:
—the true cause of division amongst men: sin—in the heart of every man, in the world's efforts;
—true unity: the salvation brought by Christ—his grace in men's hearts, his action in the world;
—the Church, bearer of this salvation, brings about the unity of this world.

Such a plan in practice would call for the use of many materials. For example the first part would call for enquiries, personal testimonies, examination of current affairs, texts from history and literature: and the second part would call for papal and patristic texts, scripture, etc.

In such a course the Epistle to the Ephesians will have its place but so will passages from profane literature such as the story of the Grand Inquisitor, or literature about the Council, or again missionary statistics.

The variety of all this material, the topical interest it has for the young people to whom we are talking and the way it is presented (analysis of texts, photocopies of documents, the first-hand experience of certain people, etc.) will all be so many elements that widen the Christian culture of the young people and at the same time enrich our catechesis.

[1] This theme can be found developed in *Catéchèse*, no. 13, October 1963, p. 461.

(b) It remains a fact that in such a course the approach is a rational approach.

From this point of view the relationship between the introduction and the facts of revelation emerges by way of reasoning. The connection between the way the young people see the world (in this case unity and division in the world, which they feel very keenly at this age) and the plan of God (who brings about unity in the Church) is made by a chain of ideas. What the young people are looking for, and the catechist with them, is a logical structure. Their knowledge of faith rests on this ordered view.

Of course this does not mean that the catechist will suggest one abstract thought after another without ceasing. The class would soon lose interest. On the contrary all the documentary material and the personal testimonies that are used will keep their interest alive and will constantly keep before their eyes concrete realities that are close to them.[1] But all this concrete material will be repeatedly taken up and reconsidered in an examination of the subject seen as a problem. They will all be treated as so many links intended to extend the chain of reflection.

This reflection will advance by the closer study of one question. Thus in the example given ("How does the Church bring about unity in the world?") the various stages of the approach could be described in this way:

—concrete facts that pin-point the problem.
—the phrasing of the question and the working out of its meaning in detail.
—the Christian answer from revelation.

[1] These will be suggested not only to the "mind" but also to the "heart". In this sense what we have to say in the following chapters about the appeal of values or the significance of a situation will have some part to play in the course of this approach. Unity is not only an idea, it is also a value. But in this case it is the "idea" that predominates.

—the consideration of the concrete facts in the light of this answer.

A schematic development in this form will never actually occur. There is bound to be a continual alternation between the various stages mentioned. But each new point will take its place in the logical structure of the problem and will make a deeper study of the question or answer possible, or it will help to show the connection between the two. This alternation between question and answer will allow knowledge to advance.

It is however always to be taken for granted that the question and the answer do in fact correspond with each other, that the Christian explanation given ("the answer") does in fact answer the "question". An approach of this nature supposes then a coherence in the chain of ideas, a coherence that can only come if one central idea is continually reconsidered, studied in greater depth and thus made more and more understandable. In the example that we have taken the whole structure rests on a certain notion, one might almost say a "definition", of unity. This is what underlies the whole course. This is the whole object of the formulation of the question, however varied that may be; and it is this idea that is made more explicit and given greater depth by all the material used in the answer given by revelation. Thanks to this same idea, continually reconsidered and studied under all its different aspects, both from the point of view of human efforts and considered as a gift of God, the connection between them is established, the "passage" is effected.

It is all rather like one of those construction kits in which one part fits into another to form a cathedral or a castle or something like that. From the moment that the very first pieces are being assembled the end must be kept in mind and each piece has its own special part to play.

This is even more true when it is a case of "building the

faith", to use an expression of St Paul.[1] With great concern for coherence (as we have just said) the actual use of this approach will call for continual reference to the norms of the knowledge of faith, if all the dangers inherent in such an approach are to be avoided.

## 2. THE ACTUAL TEACHING

When they hear the adjective "rational" mentioned, most catechists think automatically of the words "deductive" and "abstract". This is probably one of the reasons for the suspicions that we mentioned earlier. At the back of their minds there lurks the dreadful thought of that type of religious education to be found in the old classical textbooks.[2] These glories of a past age would certainly not appeal to modern youth. So this thought is firmly pushed aside, but concern for coherence and clarity is often pushed aside at the same time.

This type of "rational" teaching need not be deductive and abstract. Its object is to put before the mind a question and to give the outlines of an answer. There are however many ways of putting a question and of answering it. There are also other ways of reasoning, apart from deduction. What sort of reflection would it be if one did not take into account the concrete facts of experience, according to the old maxim *nihil in*

---

[1] Many of St Paul's arguments are similar to the approach that we have just described. To take only one example, in I Cor. 8–10 the question posed at the beginning about meat offered to idols leads St Paul to a reflection on charity and Christian freedom (based on texts and events from the Old Testament), and finally to a practical solution of the problem with which it all began. In this sense our approach could be called the "Pauline way of teaching".

[2] We have nothing against the authors of such works; they have educated generations of Christians. We can only repeat what Lesourd said about them at the Congress of Religious Teaching in 1955 apropos of first communion ceremonies at the beginning of the century: "If it succeeded yesterday, circumstances have changed .... Whatever success it had yesterday, it will not succeed today" (*Documentation Catéchistique*, June 1955, p. 67).

*intellectu quin prius fuerit in sensu* ("nothing comes into the mind without coming first through the senses")?

It is necessary to see the full scope of this "rational" approach that we are analysing. A person teaching according to this approach will be able to use a variety of ways of reasoning, but at the same time he will not reach out towards the abstract unless he is sure of a firm foundation in the concrete.

### (i) *The different ways of reasoning.*

We do not intend at this point to start a course in logic. Let us say quite simply that the teacher will be able to use all the resources of reasoning in his class.

First there is induction. From a number of facts or other documentary material the question is made clear: it is "induced" from the concrete materials used. So, in the example that we are using, it is from this yearning for unity or these signs of division in the world that we arrive at the question: "What is unity?" In this way the logical structure of the problem of unity is seen and this in its turn allows a deeper understanding of the way in which the Church brings about unity.

But in the course of a lesson many other procedures can be used. Why should deduction be left out entirely? Naturally an excess would be dangerous, and the old textbooks mentioned just now used scarcely any other method. The long chain of ideas that they built up link by link was liable to constrain the mind rather than elevate it. This is particularly true in the case of the adolescent, who likes to toy with these arguments in order to test their solidity, but abandons them the next minute for fear of becoming involved in them.

There are, then, limits to the usefulness of deduction in genuine religious knowledge. Those people who enjoy the power to build up chains of ideas must be reminded that ideas, especially religious ideas, are not meant to be juggled

34

with. The mystery of God cannot be demonstrated, and the certainty of faith is not merely the result of a logical process. This is why induction will always to some extent be preferable to deduction in religious teaching, for it proceeds from already known facts (whether from human experience or revelation), to which the mind humbly submits in order to understand them better, to see their true meaning.

There is, however, no need to be afraid of showing the adolescent who likes playing with ideas that we too can build up arguments, as well as if not better than he. And at those moments when the teacher feels that he is losing his grip on the class, because the deductive process is in full swing and moving fast with "therefore" and "because" following one another in rapid succession, there are two solutions:

(a) He can return to the concrete facts, bring an unending process to a halt and show them the great gulf between the "big ideas" and the facts with which they began and which have now been forgotten, although they are the real source of knowledge. The game comes to an end, for no longer are they juggling with abstract ideas in an unreal world; they are firmly back on earth and humbly trying to find their way.

(b) Alternatively, he can enter into the game, take it to its conclusion and then show these budding philosophers the feebleness of their efforts in comparison with the vastness of God's plan. The pride that they felt in their skill seems a little ridiculous when they turn their eyes towards heaven instead of focusing their attention on their little game. Their few ideas will take their place in a far greater complex; and even this does not exhaust the mystery of God.

Nor is this wider view to be reserved for moments of crisis. The adolescent needs syntheses, even though he may find it difficult to grasp them fully. To study a point thoroughly and to follow the slow rhythm of discovery from facts is a necessary exercise. Ideas gather weight, and in the end the words are no longer empty, but full of knowledge. From time to time there will have to be a summing-up, where deduction can be useful; for it links up ideas, but ideas that are now full of life and meaning. So, in the example suggested, when the words "unity", "Church", "world", "sin" and "salvation" have been given their full meaning, then recapitulation and synthesis become necessary. It is easy to do this by analysing the relevant passages from the Epistle to the Ephesians for example. As the various points are explained they fit into a vast pattern, and the adolescent sees in its fullness and coherence the logical structure of the problem that our catechesis was intended to show him.

Induction and deduction will, then, constantly be mixed in the course of our teaching. But there are other ways of reasoning. Analogy, comparison, paradox and contrast are some other ways open to the catechist for the advancement of the knowledge of his class. He must be able to use them and to pass from one to the other when the occasion arises. They will be useful for catechesis as long as they help in the progress towards that unified and coherent structure of the problem that we have analysed; but at the same time they must remain nothing more than aids to knowledge, used not for their own sakes but as guides in the discovery of the mystery.

### (ii) Concrete documentary material.

The same rules will be used in the choice of concrete documentary material. This is not used for its own sake but in the service of the knowledge of God; and it must figure in our teaching as something that helps the progress towards the idea, towards the logical structure of the problem.

Without labouring the point, we must be clear that by concrete documentary material we mean anything that concerns texts, testimonies, stories of real life, historical data and liturgical rites, both in the sphere of human experience and in that of revealed truth.

The first thing the catechist must ensure is that these are at the service of his teaching. Well-presented documentary material is always attractive, for in it the adolescent finds an echo of this life and this world, about which he is so eager to learn. It is an echo that is all the more attractive since it has a note of reality not possessed by ideas, for the lives of people and their problems are involved.

It is captivating, but this material can also become dominating. It can become a game like the game with ideas and arguments. No longer is it the reasoning faculty that is being tied down, but the imagination and the emotions.

Many teachers have experienced this disappointment: they thought that they were injecting new life into their classes with the introduction of documentary material, and they have come to realize that they have in fact been an obstacle rather than a help. This is often the reason for the breakdown between the point at which their interest is gained and the actual "revelation". The class has become so involved in the great mass of documentary material that they can no longer tear their imagination away in order to be able to "reflect".

What, then, is the place of documentary material in teaching according to this "rational" approach that we are discussing in this chapter?

As we have said, this approach aims at building up a coherent group of ideas. The connection between the young person's outlook on the world and the plan of God is made by way of reasoning. The documentary material is introduced in support of this reasoning; it enables the logical structure of the problem to be "induced", and it helps to give expression to the question and to give the outlines of a reply. Thus, in our example, all that the pupils have found out about unity and division leads them gradually to the question: "What sort

of unity is it that we are discussing?" Care must be taken to
see that the teacher and class do not get too involved in this
material, for that could lead to endless commentaries. The
teacher must know how to move forward, how to explain this
fact by ideas, how to relate it to other facts by means of those
points that have already been reflected on, studied thoroughly
and retained. The documentary material can only be used if
it fits into the whole structure.

Of course this must be done with great flexibility. To avoid
the danger of the documentary material occupying too important a place, it is not necessary to suppress it altogether.
And this would be the result of treating it from too rigid a
point of view, for then there would be the possibility of end-
ing up with those dreary lists of facts or texts that were the
prerogative of the old textbooks. In this way the catechesis
would again become lifeless.

But the whole point of this documentary material is to make
the class come alive. It is not possible to look at life without
being moved. So the documentary material must be allowed
to exercise all its powers of suggestion; time must be found
to enjoy it, even to reflect on it from some other point of
view. For poetry, silent contemplation and digressions of
other sorts are some of the unforeseen things that can find
a place in the religious education of adolescents. But at the
same time the catechist should be able to see beyond them
and fit them into the pattern of a far greater whole.

Sometimes someone will ask questions about a particular
piece of documentary material which are not quite to the
point. One only has to think of all that could arise in a discussion about the divisions in the world. These questions may
sometimes have nothing whatever to do with the context,
in which case they can be answered briefly. But on other
occasions they may have some indirect bearing on the subject
or they may simply be rather premature, in which case they

will have to be left unanswered and taken up again later. The adolescent will be quite ready to wait if he knows that it is not a case of avoiding a difficult question, but only of going on until it can be answered as clearly as possible.

Documentary material will, then, be introduced in order to build up the logical structure of the problem, to help to express the questions and to provide an answer. It will fit into the rational approach and support it. And from this alternation between these concrete materials and the rational structure the catechesis derives its richness.

## 3. THE ADVANTAGES OF SUCH AN APPROACH

(a) In the approach that we have just analysed the adult feels at home. In it he finds ways of thought that are familiar to him and help him (or so he thinks) to put some order into the dreadfully confused thought of the adolescent. As a teacher he will appreciate the clarity, firmness and precision which such an approach allows. It is indeed well suited to show that "coherence of mysteries" mentioned by Vatican I as one of the elements of faith. This is the first advantage of such an approach.

(b) There is a second advantage. An approach like this can be used in very different areas of religious education. To speak of a rational approach may suggest that it will be "theological" and "dogmatic". The teacher may therefore be inclined to think it best to keep this approach for the really dogmatic parts of the catechesis, that is for the explanation of the great mysteries (the Church, grace, the Trinity, etc.), while the more practical parts (the Bible, the liturgy and therefore the sacraments and salvation history) are dealt with in a different way.

But if concrete documentary material has the part to play in this approach that we have suggested, in other words if it

does in fact encourage reflection, then it is at once clear that
the rational approach can find a place in all sorts of subjects.
*A priori* no area of the Christian mystery can be excluded.
How could there be a scripture course without any reflection
on the plan of God? Or what would be the good of listing
facts about Church history or texts on social doctrine, unless
it is to see the Christian answer to our questions? There are
naturally other ways of approaching Church history and the
liturgy, as we shall show later. But many classes, biblical or
liturgical in content, will be "rational" in structure.

There is nothing wrong with this, for it is Paul's method
and the method of theology. Of course it is presumed that
the positive documentary material brought forward is left in
its original form and not reduced to a skeleton of arguments
devoid of all life, like those tedious lists in the old textbooks.

The Bible, the liturgy, in a word all the practical elements
of the Christian message, integrated in a rational structure,
all this seems to be the answer to one of the main problems
of adolescent catechesis.

It is true that old-fashioned programmes used to make
three clear divisions (dogma, sacred history and Church history), but recent studies have abandoned this threefold division. In this way catechesis has gained in quality as a result
of a greater concern for "announcing the word" and as a
result of the attention paid to the young person's outlook on
the world. But is it certain that we have not lost something
of the richness of Christian culture? The living word and
attention to the person is all very necessary. But attention to
the logical structure of problems that touch young people
should not make us forget that the reply of faith to their
question does not come from the art of reasoning or from
formulas, but from the documentary material that God himself has given to men. In other words we must integrate even
into our "rational" catecheses all the riches of the Bible and

of positive documentary material such as the liturgy. Thus it should be clear, and we want to stress this fact again, that when we speak of a "rational" approach we do not intend to reduce the catechesis to a list of dry-as-dust ideas. It simply means that the actual documents of revelation should be presented in an atmosphere of careful reflection.

Just as he is careful about the coherence of the reflection, the catechist will be careful about the richness of the material presented, in such a way that at the end of a catechetical course the young person will have a picture of the faith that is well-documented from biblical, liturgical and other sources.

The German countries distinguish between the teaching of scripture (*Bibelstünde*) and catechetical teaching in the strict sense (catechesis). In France, for administrative reasons, particularly shortage of time, there is no such distinction. This is not the place to discuss the respective merits of the two methods. But where scripture and systematic teaching are given together, it seems that the "rational approach" we have described makes possible a well-constructed catechesis which involves an awareness of the young person's view of the world and at the same time is rich in those biblical and other practical materials that are an indispensable part of Christian culture.

## 4. THE DIFFICULTIES OF THIS APPROACH

There are two in particular.

(a) This rational approach supposes a certain abstractive ability in the hearer. The mind must be sufficiently independent to see beyond the particular fact, testimony or document to the general idea.

So it will only be in the more senior classes of secondary schools that this type of approach will predominate. A few suggestions in the fifth form, but above all in the sixth form and beyond. By that time reflection is sufficiently controlled to be able to follow a chain of ideas without getting lost or becoming just silly. But it will always be necessary to have the support of concrete facts, as we have already said.

(b) The second difficulty is that such an approach is, of its nature, always in danger of destroying the sense of mystery that is an essential part of all religious education.[1] It is a question of "reflecting" and understanding rather than "contemplating" or "living". Prayer and a Christian life are in danger of being regarded as a "consequence", that is as something exterior and almost optional compared with the doctrinal aspect. This is all the more likely to be the case with the adolescent character in search of its own interior unity. A well-constructed explanation is taken as sufficient in itself, and does not lead to prayer or action.

It is in the way that he gives his teaching that the catechist will be able to avoid this mistake. The sense of mystery will appear in the respect with which he presents the documentary material and in the way in which he shows his ability to use ideas without suggesting that they are everything; in the relations that he is able to establish between the vast perspectives and the details of daily existence; and finally in the pastoral and educative atmosphere in which the catechesis takes place, making everything come alive, without itself actually being everything.

## 5. FOR THE CATECHIST

In the course of this essay we have made more than one reference to the attitude of the catechist. We now wish to

---

[1] It is particularly necessary to stress the difference between the human investigation and the gift of revelation, a difference that often shows in a sort of reversal in the procedure. In answer to the investigation of human problems we have the revelation of "the word that comes from above". There is a reversal too in the attitude of the class; after having "investigated", they must now "listen" and "accept".

stress three things that will guide him in the preparation of this sort of catechesis.

(a) In the first place there is the need to arrive at a clear formulation of the question and at the same time to give a coherent account of the answer given by faith. In other words the catechist must know what he wants to talk about and how to say it. The confusion in many cases of catechesis comes from this absence of careful attention to the details of the logical structure of the problem that is being taken as a basis for the course. Vague ideas are not enough—"Let's talk about the unity of the Church". A way must be found to go deeply into the question of what unity really is and to set out in order the main ideas on this theme. The actual course of the class may not follow the careful order of the preparation, but at least the catechist will know where he wants to go, and this is the only way of increasing the knowledge of the class. Without this clear sense of direction he will simply involve them in his own confusion.

(b) In the second place all the categories used in the analysis of the human question in the introduction must appear again, taken up in a new synthesis at the level of the response of faith. Catechesis often lacks coherence because the questions are framed in the young person's terms, while the response of faith is given in other terms, those of the catechist. The whole point of the approach we are analysing is to make both of these correspond, for it is only on these conditions that revelation can be related to the young person's outlook on the world and knowledge can progress.

(c) A lack of balance sometimes comes from another reason, and this gives rise to a third point. The question is sometimes put with a wealth of documentary material, while the answer of faith is expressed only in ideas. It should not be surprising if the first part captivates the class and the second disappoints them. An acute problem is answered in words that seem empty to them. They are not empty to the catechist, for the unity of the Church, the Mystical Body, grace, God's plan etc., are words full of meaning to him. But only too often the class will see nothing but abstract and empty ideas there. The task of catechesis is precisely to fill them with meaning by following the same procedure, which starts with the documents of revelation and ends with the formulation of the idea. The reflection of faith must therefore be "induced" from the concrete elements of revelation, just as the question was induced from the concrete elements of human experience. In this way question and answer will have the same consistency, and at the end of the course the concrete facts that were the problems (in this case the evidence of war and division etc.) will be taken up again and seen in the perspective of faith. So there will be alternation between the idea and the documentary material throughout. In this way the human question may be seen more clearly in all its detail and concrete acuteness in the light of the response of faith.

In conclusion we suggest some questions that will help to check a catechesis of this sort.

1. Has the logical structure of the problem been set out clearly?
    —can the question be framed in precise and simple terms?
    —can the answer be framed in precise and simple terms?

2. Does the logical structure of the problem shed light on the documentary material used?
    —is it plentiful enough and interesting enough (not too much and not too little)?
    —is it constantly taken up again in the light of the idea?

3. Has the answer of faith been presented in as concrete a fashion as the question?
    —is the documentary evidence of faith concrete enough?
    —has the human documentary material of the introduction been taken up again in the light of the answer given by faith?

4. Is the form of the catechesis religious enough?

Chapter Three

# The second approach:
# the "appeal of values"

When he reads this title the catechist familiar with the earlier years of adolescence will feel more at home, for the approach suggested by the title will seem closer to his normal experiences. At this age, when the love of life is so strong, surely this will be the best way of preaching the gospel message.

There are indeed advantages in this approach, but it is not without its disadvantages. Let us study it.

## I. WHAT IT IS

There is no need to define value. This is a reality that gives meaning to life and is of direct concern to the adolescent. While he is discovering all those new aspects of human life that will make him an adult, as he struggles to find his feet amidst the confusion of all his new experiences and impressions, when he feels a passionate urge to lead a full life, values appear to him like a lighthouse in a storm. To reveal to him the appeal of liberty, generosity, life, in a word the absolute value that is God, is surely to do what the gospel of the beatitudes does.[1]

This approach follows the example of the fifth chapter of St Matthew, which speaks of the desire of man for the blessings of the kingdom of heaven. On the one hand it is based on the expectations and desires of the person ("blessed") and on the other it directs this desire towards the blessings offered by the kingdom (poverty, peace, justice).

This approach, based on men's desires, starts off therefore with the spontaneous feeling which the young have for values, in order to relate these very values to God's plan. The two poles of the approach are the immediate response that the mention of values meets in the young person's mind and the blessedness to which God calls people. The connection between these two, the "passage", is made by the affirmation of one and the same value on different levels. The Call, so rich in promise yet so confused, becomes clearer and more pure all the time: it becomes the appeal of God in Jesus Christ.

An example will help to show this. Let us assume that it is a class of 13-15 year olds on the theme "God calls us to freedom".

The plan could follow this pattern:

1. Introduction: an evocative description of our desire for freedom.

2. God wants us to be free (examples, personal witness, gospel texts etc.).

[1] Just as we spoke earlier of a Pauline method of teaching, we could now speak of teaching according to the beatitudes.

3. Freedom according to God is not just any freedom.
   Our freedom is spoiled by sin.
   True and false freedom.

4. The freedom to which God is calling us is infinitely
   greater than anything that we could expect. That is
   what is meant by life according to "the freedom of the
   children of God".

The unity of such a lesson clearly comes from the affirmation of the same value ("freedom") on the different levels of
the young person's experience and of God's plan. Attracted
by the joyful call to freedom, the class will follow us as far as
the blessedness of the freedom of the children of God. Their
desire for human freedom is taken up and purified by the
revelation of freedom in Jesus Christ. In a way we are retracing
with these young people the very movement of the
sublimation of all human expectations in Christ, the movement of the redemptive incarnation. It is the same movement
and the same conditions.

These conditions could be summed up in three words:
continuity, disruption and transcendence.[1]

*Continuity:* God's call is related to the desires of our human
life. God welcomes our desires for freedom. This is a very
important point for the adolescent, who often feels that everything that goes to make up his life, all his new discoveries, are
alien to the God whose image he remembers from his childhood. He probably feels in a vague way that not everything
in his yearnings and desires is pure. To educate these feelings one must first accept them and thus guide and purify
them, not deny them. This means we must realize that every
desire for growth comes from God, for in the beginning God
created everything and it was good.

[1] Fr Babin has analysed this approach in *Orientations pour une catéchèse
des adolescents.*

*Disruption:* These feelings must be guided and purified since what was good in the beginning has been spoiled by sin. Freedom according to God is not just any freedom. The catechist's task here is to teach them to distinguish, to clear up the confusion, to help them to judge, in a word to form their conscience. And this not so much by drawing up lists of what is good and what is bad, but by showing how a clear sense of direction gives meaning to our actions. They can be judged only in relation to God's plan: a particular act of freedom is good because it fits in with the freedom of God. When we show that our desires can be in conflict with God's plan, this must not reduce us to a casuistic attitude to sin, for that would interrupt the rhythm of appeal in our catecheses. It should show that any act, however small, either leads us towards God's call to blessedness or turns us away. It is not just the fact of the conflict that is in question; it is its meaning.

*Transcendence:* "Deus qui mirabiliter creasti, mirabilius reformasti."[1] It is not so important to explain this transcendence, as to affirm it strongly. Through our desires and failures, beyond the former and in spite of the latter, God is active, calling and inviting us to happiness. It is less a theology than a mystique. The flame of our desires, which flickers and threatens to go out, can burn without restraint in the infinite. This turning to God, this certainty about his call and his assistance, are the things that guide our lives. God wants us to have real freedom and he gives it to us. A rich and imaginative approach with the help of examples from the lives of the saints, from the gospels and from the lives of Christians today, is very important for the adolescent. Frequently, what he knows is conflict, disruption. Compared with that, God's invi-

---

[1] "O God, who in a wonderful manner didst create . . . . and still more wonderfully hast renewed . . . . "—the prayer of blessing over the water at the Offertory.

tation seems lifeless. This strong affirmation, reinforced by examples, especially the personal witness of the catechist, seems all the more necessary at this point. The happiness of God, freedom according to God, these things do exist; they can crown life and give it meaning; they will never come to an end.

The actual course of the catechesis need not follow these three stages in this order. Here too there may be alternation from one to the other. Often it will be better to start with the expectations and move at once to the end (the transcendence —life in heaven), before discussing the existence of reluctance and refusal. Whatever course the explanation or dialogue may take, the important thing is that it should always be supported by the same appeal of a value. It is the same desire for freedom that, from the very beginning, attracts, strives to take shape, meets difficulties, judges which of them is a limitation and which a sin, searches hesitatingly for more light, and ends in the full light of the freedom of the children of God.

Here the metaphor is not one of building but of a living flame. The catechist's task is not to extinguish it. At the breath of the Spirit it should burn more brightly.

## 2. THE TEACHING

To make this flame burn brightly, to feed it and to guide it: these three expressions are a fair summary of what teaching according to the appeal of values should be.

To make the flame burn brightly. At the very beginning how can we suggest the key-value on which the whole catechesis depends? More simply how can we gain their interest in this matter?

To feed it. What part will documentary material play? And, as it progresses, how is it going to help the approach?

To guide it. What is the object of this approach and how is it to be achieved? In other words what are the teaching requirements of this passage to the level of the knowledge of faith in a course based on the appeal of values?

Let us discuss each of these points.

### (i) *The teaching method in the introduction.*

To live, to love, to be free, to grow—it seems easy to speak of these things to adolescents but the catechist must guard against two dangers.

If we only speak of these things in the conventional way, the words will be heard but they will be lifeless. It is possible to give a very boring class on the joys of life and love. The pupils will fall asleep or day-dream, and secretly they will feel quite frustrated.

But if the words are full of meaning, if they bring to mind things close to the life of the young, if enthusiasm can be heard in the voice of the speaker, then they will listen and in their turn will become enthusiastic. Perhaps too enthusiastic, and that is the second danger. There are certain words and certain things that are too exciting and, instead of making the class attentive and directing their minds to something beyond, they so captivate their attention that they become prisoners —prisoners of their own enthusiasm or of their own anguish. Later, if not at the actual moment, they will not be able to avoid the feeling that they have been victims of blackmail.

*Sobria ebrietas* ("sober intoxication"). This expression of the Fathers, transferred from mysticism to teaching, is perhaps the best formula for the teaching of values. In the introduction a value must be suggested in a way that rouses the imagination. It is not a question of playing with empty words, but of filling these words with all their power to arouse emotional and existential sympathy. In this matter the attitude of the catechist himself is of great importance. He is not someone on the outside, content to decide the issue from without or just to lay down the law. He is himself involved. He too is searching; he is enthusiastic, longing, meditative.... But not in any artificial way, for this is no teaching trick. God's plan is sufficiently exciting in itself to be able to do without the help of our tricks.

The catechist is also the one who can see beyond the immediate problem, the one who has already made, and whom the young people expect to have made, this connection between what enthralls them and God's plan. So this talk about values should be in an atmosphere of security, not one of blackmail. The adolescent is so aware that the passions within him are full of ambiguity that it would be as easy to make him fearful as to make him enthusiastic. The person who is also enthusiastic but can see further is not there to make life more difficult for him, nor on the other hand to fill him with false hope.

If he is ready to judge, classify, approve and condemn too hastily, if he tries to reach the goal by racing through the stages of this approach, he is in danger of spoiling it all. This shows the importance of the atmosphere at the very start of this approach.

To explain things imaginatively but soberly, in an atmosphere of attention, almost of meditation, and yet one full of life, in a way that encourages and invites further interest and does not discourage or destroy, all this takes time. A catechist in a hurry will sometimes feel that he cannot get to the religious facts quickly enough and that he is spending too much time on the "human values". But what is the good of forcing the pace, if the result is empty words? If one gives an evocative description of the values of their human lives, studying them and seeing their meaning, the fire of the Spirit is already beginning to burn in them, for they are baptized.

*(ii) The use of documentary material.*

Throughout the course this material will be used in support of this approach, but not in the way we have described for the rational approach.

The documentary material is needed in order to place the key-value in an imaginative and concrete fashion before the eyes of the class.

"To be free"—it is not so much a question of analysing the idea of freedom, as of giving an evocative description of the way freedom is lived. To be free means going out with the companion of your choice or spending your time as you like. There are times when you feel free and others when you feel constrained. Is it possible to be free and constrained at the same time? Internal freedom and external constraint? In this way it is possible to give the word freedom its widest meaning and at the same time its deepest meaning. The value of freedom is not just the absence of external force, but rather the ability to dispose oneself in one's heart. This leads the way towards the freedom of the gospels.

The documentary material, all these facts, texts, personal witness, help to make the description of the key-value really evocative. They should not be used as a basis for reasoning but for describing. The question is not "What is it?" but "When?" and "How?" These questions lead to a description of the different aspects of the value, which is open to something beyond immediate experience. So it is less the formation of a clear idea that is sought from this documentary material than the realization of the full meaning of a particular value in life. This word freedom, which is so rich in emotional content and yet so confused for the adolescent, will become a little clearer in this way and still keep its attraction.

The rational aspect is never absent in fact, or else it could not be called catechesis. But clear ideas are not the main object. It is on the emotional quality of the value that the catechesis depends. Naturally it will be necessary to put some order into what was confused, to make dividing lines clear and to find guiding lines.

To do this there will have to be some sort of rational approach, always along similar lines, the lines we defined earlier: continuity, disruption, transcendence.

But within this outline, which must be very flexible, the important thing will always be to make sure that the basic value is constantly felt as attractive and appealing.

To describe the appeal of a value and to make them hear it: in this respect the best teaching-aid is personal witness. Direct witness (of the catechist or some other person living today) or indirect witness (a gospel story or something from the lives of the saints). Witness means something directly concerning people's lives, and the main point is the attitude of these people and the choice made by them (whether it is Christ or the saints or someone living today).

One possible way would be to talk about liberty in the light of statistics about concentration camps. This will certainly appeal to feelings and imagination, but there is reason to fear that it would not affect the very centre of the free person, which is the only point at which the appeal of values can really be felt. Concentration camps are too distant and anonymous for the fifteen-year-old of today. But if he hears a description of a man forced to make a choice and torn between attraction and resistance, the adolescent will recognize himself soon enough. All the values that I long for have been sought by others too, and they have lived them to the full according to God's will. Modern Christians, the saints and Christ himself have all gone through this test of choice. They knew how to hear and follow an appeal.

Thus the flame will grow and the desire will be able to

increase, become purer and finally find its satisfaction in the happiness of God.

### (iii) *Towards the blessings of the kingdom.*

It will often be a personal testimony that will enable the link to be made between the aspirations of the young and the designs of God. This link or "passage" will be made by looking at the way some person lived, listening to his words and identifying oneself with that person. One example of course would be Christ himself, who showed himself free in relation to his family, the Pharisees and finally death itself.

This development, from the life of the young people to the plan of God, will depend throughout on the continued appeal always taken up at the different levels. This means that this development, this reflection on the value according to God, could not be made simply in the realm of ideas. The flame must be turned towards God, but in such a way that this goal should be as real and actual to the young person as the introduction was.

In one way this is not possible. The values of faith cannot have the same impact on their lives as the values of human existence, and in particular the experience the young person has of them is often poor, although it could be his good fortune to see very clearly something that familiarity will later tend to make unexciting and commonplace.

In this announcement of the values of the kingdom two dangers confront the catechist:

obvious exaggeration;

dry casuistry.

We have said that the catechist must speak of the love of God, of freedom, of the joy of God, with enthusiasm, but with an enthusiasm that is restrained and not artificial, in a tone of voice that does not too easily give the impression that it is all obvious. It is possible that the actual tone of voice or the attitude might obscure the indispensable aspect of disruption and might make them forget that this "experience of the realities of God", to use an expression of the mystics, does not affect the senses in the same way as the intense experiences of the younger adolescent.

The second danger is the extreme opposite of the first. It would be to take advantage of a captive audience in order to make them accept a boring course of casuistry at any cost. This would be another form of the "sugared pill" catechesis that we mentioned at the beginning. It is not difficult to make this mistake and the class will not always feel that they are being "blackmailed". They will be interested in knowing what is permitted and what is forbidden, but before long the words will cease to sound real and all their expectations and desires will be crushed beneath the weight of the words. No longer will it be a case of moving out into the infinity of God, but rather of not going beyond what is permitted or forbidden. In other words there will have been a change of key.

Both enthusiasm for the life of the kingdom and casuistic explanations are necessary. The catechist's task is to find the right balance between the two. To show enthusiasm and to give these explanations at the same time is not easy. The second depends on the first and care will have to be taken not to sacrifice this latter. In fact the explanations will be seen more clearly in the light of the enthusiasm. Working back from the goal will be an advantage and in the light of glory the casuistic detail can be explained. But casuistry by itself is not enough to make them appreciate what this life in God really means.

The aim of our catechesis is a religious atmosphere, rich in concrete evocative descriptions, in which these desires of the adolescent can grow into the desire for God.

59

## 3. THE ADVANTAGES OF SUCH AN APPROACH

The first advantage to be noted, although there is no need to stress it, is the fact that the appeal of values is one of the favourite ways of discovering the world at adolescence. Therefore the approach that we have described should be one of the best forms of catechesis for this age-group.

In this approach the views that the young person is in the process of forming, about the world and about himself, are related to God's plan. Instead of turning in on itself in a wild passion, this desire for life goes beyond itself and enters into the real fullness of life.

Such an approach allows us to reassure the adolescent about the whole of life. By going through all the great values of his life with him we can gradually relate the whole of his existence to the plan of God.

There is less to fear if human life and the knowledge of faith are seen to be closely related. The discussion of values allows the deepest understanding of this existence, which is in the process of formation. There is less risk of learning and behaviour staying in separate compartments. The teaching itself links up the human and the Christian, and it avoids that division between ordinary life and religion that paralyses so many Christian lives.

The second advantage seems to be that this approach is also the best when the discussion is about morals. Any genuine moral catechesis like the one described is not content to give casuistic explanations; it reveals the intentions behind Christian action. It is a catechesis of the spiritual life, of life according to God. To study the main values of the adolescent's life is also to study the great aspects of human life and therefore the main aspects of Christian morality. In this perspective it should be possible to work out a programme, which from the adolescent's point of view is an evocative description of all that arouses his attention and enthusiasm, and at the same time from the point of view of revelation is a lesson on all the great problems of morality.

But clearly such a perspective allows an approach to many other subjects apart from morality. Since it concerns God in so far as he is happiness for us, it is the whole mystery of God that opens up before us: the last things, the sacraments, the Church or the life of the Trinity, as well as morals in the strict sense.

Once again we are faced with the fact that in our catechesis we cannot separate things that are legitimately distinguished from the theological point of view. In fact this is not an analytical view but a synthetic reflection, since it is a question of relating the knowledge and the life of a being in the process of formation. Thus around the theme "God wants us to be free" all sorts of ideas and texts may be gathered, about heaven, the place of freedom, or the religious life and examples of true freedom. It must be repeated that these points are not joined together by logical thought but by an evocative description of the same basic value. We may also point out that this appeal of values will often be used together with other types of approach. The unity of the Church for example can scarcely be analysed without the word unity becoming a value that attracts, at the same time that it is becoming clearer as a concept.

## 4. DIFFICULTIES OF SUCH AN APPROACH

It carries with it its own limitations. The appeal of the beatitudes moved the crowds. But when the emotion of the first days of the Galilean ministry died down and when the "ascent to Jerusalem" appeared on the horizon, how many abandoned Christ! "Blessed" indeed, but with a happiness

c

that is achieved by way of the cross. This was already present in the earliest preaching, but many never saw it and remained in ambiguity.

It may be the same with the adolescents. The first danger of such an approach is this persistent ambiguity about the values being discussed. To live, to be free, to grow—the catechist will gradually explain and show the demands contained in God's plan, but the explanations will be unexciting beside the emotional power unleashed in the first stage of evocative description.[1] From this to what the learned call "immanentism" is only one step.

This danger does exist, but to criticize an approach that is one of the great gospel approaches and the approach of a whole spiritual tradition does not mean that we have to reject it. It is precisely in the use of the approach that care is needed in order to keep a balance. This is achieved much more by the quality of the personal testimonies (both of joy and of the cross) than by any logical construction, which has no effect on the class at all.

This is the second danger. Even if there is no ambiguity about the values suggested as far as the gospel is concerned, a lack of balance can appear between the first stage of our teaching (the evocative description of the value in the life of the young people) and the last stage (this same value in God's plan)—a lack of balance that comes from treating one in a realistic fashion, with a wealth of documentary material (which is very interesting), and presenting the other in the form of an idea. Unobtrusively there is a change of key. The adolescent feels that human freedom is real and exciting, while freedom according to God is a matter of words. The catechesis then seems to him like a form of "blackmail" on his good in-

---

[1] This approach is in itself "a-historic"; it is directed towards the realization of an ordeal rather than towards salvation in event. It is difficult for it to avoid anthropocentrism or "theism".

tentions (it might even look like sharp practice). He feels that he has been misled by this evocative description of life just to make him swallow the bitter pill of the old commandments. But these will only be acceptable to him if he sees them in the light of the new life present for him in the testimonies and other documentary material close to him. The catechist must imitate the scribe in the gospel who brings out of his treasure "both new and old".

There is a third difficulty. Even if, in the depths of his heart, the adolescent hears this call to a decision and to a life according to God, it is not easy in such a catechesis to explain it in terms of knowledge. Generosity can inspire enthusiasm, but there may be only a dim realization of its real meaning. On the other hand to try to reason about it may only cause the class to lose interest. Or else they might only be interested in the casuistry, in the exterior and moral aspect of the message, without accepting its theological content. It is difficult to keep this balance in a catechesis that depends all the time on the appeal of values, trying to relate them to all the richness of God's plan in a clear and evocative manner, without becoming mere casuistry.


## 5. FOR THE CATECHIST

This approach can lead more easily than any other to the danger of demagogy. Even if he is deceived for the moment, the adolescent will not readily forgive the trick, which he is bound to discover sooner or later. He will not be proud to think that he has been duped and it is even possible that he may take his revenge on the subject-matter of the teaching and not only on the catechist himself.

Two things will help the catechist to avoid such a disaster happening to him.

In the first place he must show great concern for the truth, not only in what he says but also in the way he says it. It is too easy to play on the feelings of a young audience for him to abuse this power. God's truth is too moving in itself for us to feel any need to make a travesty of it with our cheap tricks.

In the second place, in the actual course of the catechesis we must give full attention to the aspect of disruption. Man's progress towards the new life and blessings of the kingdom had been spoiled by sin. The place of sin must be stressed and so must the fact that it is only a total opening out in hope that will not lead to pessimism. For sin cannot be discussed without any mention of salvation. Such a lesson follows the actual pattern of creation, sin and new creation. The second aspect then must not be exaggerated nor must it be eliminated.

In conclusion we suggest some questions that the catechist can ask himself in the case of a catechesis of this sort.

1. Has the central value been made clear enough?

2. Has it been described in an attractive way, in a way that is meaningful for young people, with plenty of documentary material:
   —in its human aspect;
   —as far as Christian life is concerned?

3. Has it been made clear enough from the point of view of the knowledge of faith:
   —with regard to the actual value in question;
   —with regard to the casuistic explanations for the life of the young people?

4. Has each of the three aspects (continuity, disruption and transcendence) been given its rightful place in the catechesis?

Chapter Four

# The third approach:
# the meaning of a situation

There seems to be yet a third way for the catechesis of adolescents. This starts from an analysis of the situations that they meet. It is less abstract than the appeal of values and seems to contain what is best in both the other approaches.

## 1. WHAT IS IT?

In front of his class the catechist is like Christ in front of those who came to him. Contact often appears superficial, and the topics for discussion seem to be only things of an immediate interest, such as something in the news, some class escapade or some other aspect of the young people's lives, some particular problem or question or piece of advice.

The Samaritan woman talked of water and of the well, and

the man born blind had only one problem: he wanted to be able to see.

Yet in welcoming them Jesus saw further than they. Their hope for water or for a cure, which was their only preoccupation, concealed and at the same time revealed some deeper hope and desire, the desire for living water and for the light of the world. They were only superficially aware of their own situation: Christ revealed it to them in all its depth. What they considered a passing thirst or a particular need was nothing other than the expression on the conscious level of a deeper thirst, the infinite desire for the kingdom of God. Their gestures, words and relationships all took on a new meaning. From this moment on they were and they acted like men "saved".

This approach based on the meaning of a situation follows the pattern of the Gospel of St John.[1] Like Christ, the catechist is the one who can see farther and who knows how deep the thirsts and desires of the young people really are. It is his task to show them the deeper meaning of their own desires. They only see themselves and the world and the people round them in a superficial way, while the true meaning of their situation escapes them. So the catechesis shows them how things that were seen as superficial in their existence are in fact of deep meaning, and of significance for the kingdom of God. In this way the young person's way of looking at the world, and all his hopes and desires, are related to the Christian message. The idea then is to take a situation and find the total meaning by which it is related to the plan of God.

Take for example a class for adolescents of 13–15 years on the theme "God invites us to share his love". It could be along the following lines.

[1] Just as we spoke of "Pauline teaching" or "teaching according to the beatitudes", we can speak here of "Johannine teaching".

1. Introduction: our encounters with others. They may be superficial or they may affect us in the very centre of our being.
2. God is inviting us to an encounter—with himself:
   —today (the witness of converts);
   —Jesus meets Zacchaeus;
   —Elijah and Moses.

There is no human loneliness that cannot find solace in God. Salvation is an encounter with God. On what conditions?

3. The Christian is the one who has this encounter with God, and then reflects it and makes others share it. We meet God in others, and in the Mass, which is a meeting with Christ. In our human encounters too God is present.

The following remarks can be made about this form of catechesis.

(a) It is difficult to classify. In content it is dogmatic, moral, sacramental and spiritual. Rather like the gospel story of the Samaritan woman or the man born blind, it contains the mystery of God, the sacraments and human conduct all together. Nor is this synthetic view too much for the adolescent. On the contrary it brings to life those things that had been dormant in him up to this point, relating one to another in a way that is surprising but nonetheless vital. Encounters with others, a matter that is a cause of great joy or sorrow in his daily life, takes on a new meaning, for to meet another is to meet God in the other. Such a catechesis has a profound unity, and by this very unity it enriches the mind and the heart.

(b) In order to analyse its development more closely, it could be described in three stages.[1]

---

[1] We emphasise that these "stages" are logical stages and that the catechesis will not necessarily follow this order in actual practice.

The introduction is a situation, some aspect of the adolescent's existence. In this case it is meeting others. This must be studied and described, not only by drawing up lists of ideas or looking for values in it, but by trying to see in it the profound significance for us. To meet others is to alternate between loss of self and withdrawal into oneself. Our situation is ambiguous. What meaning does our existence have?

Secondly the introduction is developed. The lives of modern Christians or of the saints and the Bible give us many examples of this meeting of God and men. In the gospels Christ met situations similar to ours. We could examine for example the circumstances in which he met Zacchaeus, and see how this meeting was for Zacchaeus a completely new opening, and at the same time the rejection of an aspect of his life that had been wrong. We find the same things in our encounters: total openness to "the one that comes to meet us" and the renunciation of everything in us that is an obstacle to this meeting.

In the third place there must be a summing up. God gives meaning here and now to our lives. He does for us what he has done throughout the history of salvation. Our Christian existence today is related to revelation, and the life we live now is what the Bible, the liturgy and Church history tell us about.

(c) We must now see what it is that gives unity to this catechesis.

It is clear that it proceeds by putting situations side by side, comparing our situation to those of other Christians, the saints, people in the gospel or in the Old Testament. In this sense it studies events from different moments of history from the same point of view and shows their unity. It follows the pattern of salvation history itself. What God does for us today is what he did for his people in the past: God's ways are always the same.

As far as the teaching is concerned, the unity between these different situations (the modern situation, expressing the young people's outlook on their world and all their hopes and desires, and the situation of salvation-history, revealing God's plan) is achieved by taking up the same theme at different levels. In this case the theme is encounter with others. It is from this point of view that the human situation and the gospel situation are compared. An evocative description of the different situations is possible, and at the same time the progression from one level to the other. Around this theme the human experience of the adolescent gradually crystallizes and in its light they learn to see some of the facts of their existence in a much more profound way. Friendship, loneliness, team-work, arguments, are all a question of the success or failure of encounters. This same theme also helps us bring together the documentary material of revelation, to see how God takes human encounters and makes them the meeting-place of his own love. The theme is the axis of this approach, combining all the warmth of human experience and also all the life of God's plan. In short, this approach according to the "significance of a situation" means that we explain the unique situation of human existence in the light of the unique significance of God's plan.

## 2. THE ACTUAL TEACHING

Throughout this type of approach the one object will be to bring together in their burning actuality all the aspects of human life in order to make the love of the Trinity grow there.

There are some important points to be noted.

(i) *In the introduction an evocative description of the situation of the young person must be given.*

Not in itself: this is not a case of analysis or diagnosis, but of helping the boys and girls in their own language to realize the full meaning of some aspect of their lives. There are two questions that should help the catechist:

—What are the important aspects of life for them?

—How do they express these among themselves?

What does it mean to a 15 or 18 year-old "to live" or "to grow up"? It means passing exams, going camping, going out in groups, day-dreaming and listening to records, loving, making things, etc.

We often speak to them about their problems and all the good textbooks have chapters on matters like the relationship between boys and girls, friendship or the work of Christians in the world. Why then is it that we so often have the feeling that it is all to no avail? To the ones that listen it is just a matter of words, lifeless, distant words, while deep down within them the passionate love of life continues to grow, unmoved by our words, which seem to be quite beside the point. They do not see, they often do not even imagine, that there can be any connection between what we are saying and their innermost selves. As with two friends trying to say something to each other through a barrier of glass, our efforts to communicate soon become mere grimaces. Our clumsy efforts to play at being teenagers just make them laugh. If we try over much to adapt, our catechesis becomes inconsistent.

This barrier must be penetrated. Our efforts at sympathy, which is essential to all real communication and education, must help them to express to themselves, and together with the teacher, what their life really means. For they do not know themselves what they really are. With a mixture of fear and fascination they allow themselves to be carried away by this inward urge, without ever learning to control it. That is why words that just classify and arrange mean nothing to them.

It must be in their own words, experiences and feelings of sympathy, however limited they may seem to us, that we help them bit by bit to express their outlook on the world for themselves. Thus pop singers and television will find a place in our catechesis. But did the water in Jacob's well have "in itself" any greater interest? This is not a case of *captatio benevolentiae,* not a question of capturing their interest just to lead them on to something else. The whole point is to help them to express to themselves the full meaning of their life, their situation in existence, in relation to other beings and other things, and this in their own words and symbols.[1]

The teacher is no longer a 16 year-old. He may have a gift for this type of reflection or he may not. They do not expect us to be as knowledgeable as themselves about pop music or film stars, but they do want to be accepted, to be able to express their way of looking at things to themselves and to others. What if we do hear in our classes such remarks as "It reminds you of that film . . ." or "That record makes you think". It is a good thing that it should be so. It is a sign that our teaching has penetrated to the depths of their being.

*(ii) To see the situation in all its "scope" and "depth".*

We must not only accept and give an evocative description of the young people's way of looking at things. We must also help them to see it in context and thus to transcend it and see its deepest significance.

To see its full context. The context of a situation is bigger than the individual; it includes others, it includes the world. Around an individual experience we must show the far wider circle of human experiences. Others have also experienced what it means to meet people. About us and before us others have known what friendship means. In the same words, but

---

[1] Different procedures are possible: either to start directly from the situation of the young person (some fact or reflection); or to start from a testimony in which he will recognize himself; or to speak in what seems to be a general way, but in his own words, particularly his own symbolic expressions.

also with other words, they have expressed their experiences. The adolescent will identify himself with these "witnesses", who are more or less close to him (according to his age and abilities), in whom he recognizes himself and who provide him with a language in which he can express his own experiences. He can see himself as a modern pop singer, then why not as St Francis or St Paul? This examination of the wider context of the situation by setting it alongside other situations will also help us to see it in greater depth.

To study it in depth. Now he will begin to choose his words more carefully: bit by bit, "his own words" will begin to be related to the words of ordinary language, and his attitudes will be explained with universal symbols, and these will be filled with the weight of original experience. Thus the situation with which the class began will become more objective. What was seen as something essentially individual will become related to the experience of others, and so to society and its objective norms.

Then he will be able to see a new "meaning" in his own experience and his own situation. No longer will he ask "What is it?" or even "How and when?" but "Why?" and "What is the meaning of that?" The evocative description of his situation is not an ordinary description or an analysis. By a thorough investigation it makes all his own tendencies more understandable. The limited or superficial aspects, with which a start had to be made, give way to a more profound questioning. Beyond matters of detail the catechesis reaches the profound question. Wherever a start is made, this study in depth relates things to the basic questions of man about himself and his life, to which God's plan gives meaning.

*(iii) To reveal the Christian significance of the situation.*

We should not delay unduly over the wider context and depth of the situation. It is after all Jesus Christ who gives meaning to all the hopes, desires and experiences that make up human existence. To state this fact is not enough. We must show how God takes human history and turns it into sacred history.

Today:

This is a stage with which we must deal fully. Events in the Old Testament or even the gospels are far removed in time and often in language. The indispensable link is the Christianity of today. Other young people, men and women, living in the same world and time as ourselves, meet the same situations and find a way of meeting God in all this. This is a point at which personal testimony is very valuable, the testimony of militant Christians, of converts, of saints whose lives bear some resemblance to the lives of the adolescents, of a Christian life in ordinary conditions, of the Church in the world and finally of the catechist.

It should not be difficult to see the point of all this. It is to show how an existence as "incarnate" as that of the adolescent can still be part of God's plan. It is not just an appeal then, for in one sense the greater the distance, the stronger the appeal. On the contrary it is a reflection based on things around them. They are the "same" but in a different way.

Understood in this way the place of topical matters in adolescent catechesis presents no difficulties. Things of immediate interest in their experience (the latest newspaper article or film, for example) will be better understood in the light of the reality of the mystery of God, present today in his witnesses. This will not always be easy, for it is more difficult to give an evocative description of a religious reality than of a profane matter. After all, religious realities are God's secret. And the documentary material that we have at our disposal is not always well designed from this point of view. There are not many saints' lives that show God acting today in a language easily understood by the young.

It calls for imagination on the part of the catechist, but also for care. Before any class he should ask himself: "In their experience what are the signs of God's plan, the signs of the Church, that are within their grasp?" Their faith rests on the signs of today,[1] and it is these signs that will allow them to grasp the signs of salvation-history, above all *the* sign, who is Jesus Christ.

In salvation history:

The situations of the young people, the situations of other Christians today, the normative situations of salvation-history: these are the three stages. In the actual course of the catechesis they will perhaps be mixed. The last stage must on no account be left out, for it alone allows us to build up a coherent and ordered view of the faith, and therefore enables us to organize our teaching.

On the superficial level there is no resemblance between the situations of life today and those in the gospel. In scripture you will find neither pop music nor films. But as we have seen already, many aspects of the life of the young people are only an expression of a deeper existence, to which scripture alone can give any meaning. On every page of scripture we read of encounters, of joy, of the search for God, of life in the company of others, of longing for the kingdom, or even of loneliness. The adolescent will not be able to see this at once, and will be likely to say: "Oh, the gospels!" because it will bring back childhood memories of catechism classes, and memories that might even be unhappy ones. He must be taught to read the gospel and the whole of the Bible with new eyes and in all its human depth.

There is no need to overwork the text or to make any artificial paraphrases. Simply let them learn to read it, stress

[1] Amongst these a special place will be given, apart from personal witness, to the sacraments, in which the history of salvation actually takes place. Receiving the faith is not only the "discovery" of certain knowledge, it is an "initiation" into the life of the community of salvation.

any words that are at all likely to remind them of their experiences, and look for the great symbolic attitudes: the looks of Christ and his encounters, the dreams and disappointments of the apostles, the boldness of the prophets. Understood in all their living reality these will make this once again "the book of life".

To make a stereotyped expression come to life again it will be enough to say it again, to "retranslate" it, in the language of modern youth.

We are not looking for "good examples" in the people we meet in scripture, but for beings full of life, people who have known our longings and enthusiasms and have filled them with God.[1] That is how they will have to be described, from inside as it were, from their own point of view.

God and Christ will become real persons, precisely in the degree that they are related to the young person at the centre of his existence, in those situations that are his own.[2]

## 3. THE ADVANTAGES OF THIS APPROACH

(a) It is possible to give an evocative description of a situation in various ways and with different words. Here it will be enough to stress the importance of symbolic language in this approach.

"Symbols give food for thought." This is a saying that appealed to Ricoeur[3] and it seems the key to the approach that we are discussing.

[1] What has been called "hero pedagogy" (as analysed by Bournique, Soffray and Pilet) seems to depend on this approach. The situation of the young person is directly related to the situations in the Bible by the language used and the way of presenting the particular character in the situations with which the young person identifies himself (cf. *La pédagogie du héros*, in the collection "*I.S.P.C. Ecole de la Foi*", ed. Fayard-Mame).

[2] We have not written a special paragraph about the use of documentary material. This approach rests entirely on such material and even more on the way it is used, as we have already described in the preceding chapters.

[3] *Finitude et culpabilité*, vol. 2, p. 26.

No one's life and experiences, let alone those of an adolescent, can be expressed in just any language. The best way is the language of symbols. We must repeat that it is not a case of explaining or analysing, but of describing in an evocative manner, in the young person's own way, in his own words and attitudes; in short we must use his own symbolism.

They live more from symbols than ideas. We have only to hear them talk, or read what they write, to see springing up at every moment images that really are full of life. Any proclamation of the faith that hopes to affect their lives cannot afford to ignore such language. This is all the more important, since this is the language of the Bible, of the liturgy and of the experience of the Church. This is the first advantage of such an approach. Developed in a study of the significance of the situation it will make it possible to come into much closer contact with the existence of the person concerned, and with the support of these symbolic themes to read its significance in all its human and Christian depth. There will be a reciprocal movement between the symbol and the idea, and between experience and knowledge.

But it may be objected that there is here a danger of reducing the catechesis to a mere game with images, to a collection (and not a very good one) of real-life stories.

(b) Such an objection would reveal a misunderstanding. A catechesis of this sort is not just a matter of luck. On the contrary it has a very clear structure: its development is the development of salvation-history itself. This is the second advantage to be noted.

God's plan, as realized in Jesus Christ, actually touches us in the life of the Church today.[1] The teaching approach that we have outlined consists simply in going through these three points: from the "today" of my existence to Jesus

[1] Cf. *Catéchèse*, no. 3: "Le carrefour sur l'histoire du salut"; no. 1: "L'histoire du salut au coeur de la catéchèse" (P. Biard).

Christ and to God. The things that happen in everyday life are not studied in their superficial detail, nor is the catechesis a collection of anecdotes. The significance of the situation is deepened until its relation to the plan of God is seen. Such an approach aims right at the heart of human hopes and at the same time right at the heart of the plan of salvation. Does this mean that we have to try to relate something like a modern dance to the Trinity? Why not? Christ after all started from a pitcher of water to show the love of the Father.

Understood in this way this approach means that we are getting to the heart of the Christian mystery, precisely as it has been revealed, in the experience of the People of God, in the experience of Christ, in the experience of the Church's tradition. After that it is easy to add a word or two about the intellectual or moral point of view. But the danger of being left with an intellectual or casuistic construction has been avoided. Reflection on situations and experience, both of the young people and of the People of God, leads to action as well as ideas; it invites us to act and to be, as well as to understand. As we pointed out at the beginning in the discussion about the catechesis of encounter, this is dogmatic as well as moral, liturgical and spiritual.

## 4. THE DIFFICULTIES OF THIS APPROACH

This combination of different areas of religious knowledge, which is a blessing for catechesis, is a source of difficulty for the catechist. Familiar categories will be difficult to recognize. He will be required to show great flexibility and at the same time great doctrinal ability, both in working out the course and in putting it into practice.

### (i) *The planning of programmes.*

It is easy to work out a programme in the framework of

theology, for chapter headings and connections are ready made. But when we try to include the living concerns of our pupils, this fine order is disturbed.

One extreme would be to do this only as the occasion arose, that is, to be satisfied with an explanation of the immediate aspects of experience without bothering about any coherent sequence.[1] This would not be enough. Even if it only deals with the deepest experience, as we have said, going beyond superficial questions to the great hopes of the adolescent and of all men, it will not be easy to arrange a programme. Any profound human question (e.g. the one under discussion, our meeting with others) brings up the whole of God's plan; the Trinity, the incarnation, the redemption, the Church, the sacraments: everything can come in here.[2] To work out a programme from these points of view calls for particular care about two points: coherence from the point of view of the subject and coherence from the point of view of the doctrine. If this seems difficult, the fault probably lies in the lack of sufficient reflection both about the depth of the significance of human experience at any given moment in the life of a person, and about the corresponding depth of the significance of God.

*(ii) Putting this approach into practice.*

This approach can be used in many different ways. Since it consists in building up a catechesis out of the adolescent's way of looking at the world, as he expresses it to himself, in order to relate it as closely as possible to the plan of God, it can be used at different age-levels.[3] But obviously a 17 year-

[1] An experience can be interpreted in many ways. Symbols always have more than one meaning; they are polyvalent.

[2] The approach that we have analysed is not unlike the "review of life" in Catholic Action. But the catechesis is different from this since it is guided by the need for coherence in the doctrinal explanation and is not simply used to explain some occasional event.

[3] This is also useful in the case of small children or adults.

old's outlook on the world will not be the same as that of a 14 year-old. So the same approach can appear outwardly very different at times. To take an example: the "hero pedagogy" about which we were talking earlier is one form of this approach, the one best suited to pre-adolescence. But it should not be difficult to imagine other forms for different age-groups and with different themes. It seems that one of the tasks of religious education is to work out in a concrete fashion catecheses of this type for the various stages of adolescence.

## 5. FOR THE CATECHIST

There is one fundamental point that must be stressed. We must learn to express the Christian message in terms that are the terms of experience, without being false either to the experience of the young people or to the richness and clarity of experience in the Church or the Bible. The greatest difficulty that the catechist starting this course will come across comes precisely from lack of practice in anything other than dogmatic language, or on the other hand from lack of consistency, when everyday life is taken as the starting-point. But it is possible to reveal all the riches of doctrine in a lively way and at the same time to treat of life in a consistent way. It is only care for these two points that will give the catechist flexibility and also security in such classes. Symbols will no longer be just "pictures" and the evocative description of experience will no longer be a mere catalogue of different facts. It must be realized that "symbols do give food for thought".[1]

In short then it means learning how to pass on the "living word" to "living people".

[1] This presumes reflection on Christian anthropology, which is the very basis of the teaching that we have explained.

*Some questions for a catechesis of this sort.*

1. Has the central doctrinal theme been related to a human situation of the class?

2. Has a sufficiently evocative description of this situation been given? How? With what symbols or words etc.?

3. Has the biblical documentary material, and anything else used, been allowed to shed light on the meaning of this situation? How has it been used?

4. Has the catechesis been sufficiently well constructed? Rich enough from the doctrinal point of view? Clear enough?

5. Has it opened up possibilities for action? Christian witness, sacramental life etc.?

# Conclusion

Anyone who has followed our essay up to this point will still probably have some questions to ask.

It must be said at once that any attempt to forecast the actual course of a lesson is bound to be a failure, at least to some extent. Life can be analysed and described, but words can never represent it in all its complex simplicity.

We have chosen the path of analysis, since in the case of the adolescent the path of description only seems possible at particular points. In an attempt to be really practical, we suggest here in the conclusion certain things to which attention must be paid.

(i) *The approaches as analysed never exist in their pure state.*

What we have done is a sort of "radiography". Under very different forms certain "types of structure" keep on appearing in adolescent catechesis, types that are seen as so many ways of relating the world of the young person to the world of faith.

But it is quite clear that the rational approach will always include some appeal to values or some reflection on existence, just as ideas will always be in the background of any teaching according to values or the significance of a situation.

One or the other, however, will predominate. Thus it is important for the catechist to realize what key he has chosen. If he does, he will be able to do certain things.

Firstly he will be able to see the key points in the course of his catechesis (the questions that we have drawn up at the end of each chapter are a sort of catalogue of the important points). They will also indicate a certain order, although it is not possible to fix this order absolutely.

Secondly he will be in a position to avoid that frequent discrepancy that we mentioned in the first chapter, between the starting-point at which the attention of the young people is gained and the actual presentation of the facts of faith. We have also pointed out one or two other causes of this break-down in the course of this essay. Now we have to mention one more. This comes from presenting the introduction (the point at which the attention and interest is gained) in one key (that of values or existence) and the Christian reply in another key (that of ideas).

Finally, one means of holding the class's attention will often be to switch from one approach to another, to encourage rational reflection by appealing briefly to values or the analysis of a situation, and vice versa.

(ii) *How to use these different approaches according to the different aspects of the content of faith.*

Can we say that there is any one aspect of revelation that corresponds to a particular approach? For example, does dogma correspond to the rational approach, morals to the approach of the appeal of values, and the sacramental world to the approach of the significance of a situation?

Absolutely speaking the answer is in the negative. The whole of revelation (dogma, morals and sacraments) can be expressed either in ideas or in life-values, or according to the real life situations (for example from the Bible).

But it is still true that, especially for adolescents, each of the approaches can be suited to some particular aspect of faith.[1] This is most clear in the teaching of morality according to the approach of the "appeal of values". In the same way the sacraments can be very well explained if they are taken as situations of existence, rather than analysed as ideas.

It would be worth-while to see how other areas of religion, especially apologetics, can be based on one or other of the approaches suggested, in the case of adolescent catechesis.

*(iii) The approaches at the different stages of adolescence.*

In the course of this essay we have already said that the rational approach seems best if reserved for later adolescence, while the appeal of values appears ideal at the age of puberty.

On the other hand the third approach, which can take many forms in practice, seems to us to be suitable for all ages. The manner of the approach will differ, since the situations of the young people differ and so do their ages. The "hero pedagogy" is one of the forms suited to programmes for pre-adolescence. But other forms can very well be used in the second and third stages of adolescence. They need to be more carefully built up from the point of view of ideas, especially in later adolescence, but it will still be a question of relating the situation of the adolescent to the normative situations of salvation-history, even if they are now more cap-

[1] To pursue this question would require reflection on the various logical forms in which tradition has expressed the revealed message.

able of reflecting on this relationship and expressing it in ideas.

The task of the catechist is to choose the approach that suits his particular class. He must combine the various approaches in order that the young people's outlook on the world, their expectations and their opportunities for action may be thoroughly filled with the spirit of the gospel.